IDENTITY DISCOVERY

"The Awakening of the Apostolic"

Written By: Derry L. Haywood III

Write It Out Publishing LLC Assisted.

ISBN: 979-8-9919982-7-7 (Paperback)
ISBN: 979-8-9919982-8-4 (eBook)

Book Cover Illustrator: Derry L. Haywood III
Editor: Derry L. Haywood III

First printing, (e-book or paperback) December 2025
Derry L. Haywood III
Richmond, Virginia
innovate@embracetheliberty.org

Ezra 3:10 *"Now when the builders had laid the foundation of the temple of the Lord, the priests stood in their apparel with trumpets, and the Levites, the sons of Asaph, with cymbals, to praise the Lord according to the directions of King David of Israel."*

Exodus 35:31 *31 The LORD has filled Bezalel with the Spirit of God, giving him great wisdom, ability, and expertise in all kinds of crafts.*

Table of Contents

Endorsement Collective

I have sat under the teachings of Pastor Derry Haywood III for more than 10 years during the annual prayer gatherings and leadership trainings by Dorcas Enterprise Ministries. As a prayer leader with Alabaster Women's Ministries, I have discerned his highly anticipated sermons and lectures as revelatory and prophetic. But this new work, "Identity Discovery: The Apostle...God's Architect", reveals Pastor Haywood's elite mastery in the study of God's plan that - when read and received - could catapult individual Christians worldwide into their divine callings. Whether being read and studied for Christian growth or enjoyed by anyone simply for educational purposes, this anointed book is truly groundbreaking and a blessing to the body of Christ.

Elder Hazel Trice Edney,
founding president, Alabaster Women's Ministries; President/CEO, Trice Edney Communications; Editor-in-Chief, Trice Edney News Wire.

Pastor Derry Haywood III is a covenant co-labor in the Kingdom of God with me here on Earth. Over the years, I have observed his "YES" to whatever God has for him to accomplish through this one statement, "I endeavor to do all I can do for the Lord, in an Excellent Spirit." (Daniel 5:12) I believe this Book, "Identity Discovery" will encourage, inspire, and evoke deeper thought and a spiritual "Go" within you to embark upon your own identity discovery journey. So, I encourage you to join the journey, enjoy this read. Invest in discovering your predestined Kingdom assignment here on earth.

Apostle Audrey Newell M.A./M.Div.
Dorcas Enterprise Ministry

Pastor Derry Haywood is a phenomenal trainer and teacher. Identity Discovery will be a vital asset to the people of God. Pick up your copy today!

Apostle Mike Hathaway,
New Generation Church RVA

"Thought provoking, transformative, anchoring... Pastor Derry Haywood has created a literary masterpiece that you're going to have trouble putting down. This book is a necessary manual for the modern day apostolic builder. Soaked in revelation and divine wisdom, each page will open the eyes of the builder to see themselves the way God saw them at the moment of creation. Prepare to build with clarity and courage as you unlock God's premeditated purpose and plan for your life."

Prophetess Ciara Mason,
Founder of Razing Women

Identity is important, especially for Kingdom citizens. If you don't know who you are, you can't understand your Kingdom assignment, mandate, and mission, nor how you are to operate in them to advance the Kingdom for the glory of God.

In this book, my brother, friend, and true Kingdom and Apostolic ambassador, Pastor Derry Haywood, III, outlines for us in Identity Discovery how to identify who you are based on the Master Architect's plans. He reminds us that we entered the earth with everything we needed. We were born in the image and likeness of the One who knew us before we were us. Here we stand because of predestination, with the full rights, power, and authority of one who is a Kingdom Ambassador for the King of kings.

I highly recommend you read Identity Discovery so that you, too, fully understand your identity has nothing to do with you; it was predetermined by the One who foreknew you, the Master Architect with the perfect plan. He's simply waiting for you to say yes. When you do, He will bring to earth what He's already done in heaven.

Elder Angela Thornton,
Wise Word Ministries

Dedication

I would like to dedicate this writing to some important people who have gone to be with God but their impact in my life is everlasting.

- Dr. Christina Rouson, God used you to love me from a broken place. You spoke life to me and I began to live again.
- Elder Gloria B Collins, you cultivated the gift of intercession within me and taught me the value of prayer
- Elder Cassie Penn, my spiritual midwife and prayer partner…only God knows the love I will always carry in my heart for you!
- Kim Hobson Bell, my "Mother in Love"…thank you for always loving me as your son, I will forever cherish our private chats.

With Gratitude...

I truly believe we are the sum total of all of our experiences in life. Within those experiences we meet people who would help to shape the framework of who we are and those unlocking our potential and destiny. I would like to take this opportunity to thank a few of the people who have been instrumental in making this journey possible.

1. My first pastors: Dr Sharon Riley and Dr Barbara Amos, thank you for the foundation in God and excellence that you provided, I'm grateful for your teachings.

2. My "midwives" are those who taught me the language and posture prayer. Thank you Betty Temple, Malisia Lee, Elaine Little, and Renee Bristol who armed me with the baptism of the Holy Spirit. I will always honor you for that.

3. To a special surrogate mother, Audrey Hatfield, thank you for your unconditional love and consistency over the years. Your labor of love has not gone unnoticed and it can never be forgotten.

4. To my church, Freedom House RVA, thank you for the support and love for me over the years. We have seen many battles but we have seen even greater victories. One Way Churches International, Bishop Lorenzo Hall and Bishop S.Y. Younger thank you for your unparalleled leadership and covering.

5. Brothers who pushed me: Prophet Alec, God knitted us for this Apostolic Journey and I'm so thankful he did. Pastor Cedric Rouson, we did church planting 101 together at the kitchen table many days. Thank you for your brotherhood. Pastor Sterling Burton, you have

been a Godsend thank you for what we share…one word sums it up…"Covenant." Lastly, Ali Rezahi, thank you for challenging and pushing me in the Marketplace…I'm a far better leader because of you. Thank you my friend.

6. To My Sisters, Shirvelle, Sonja, Sherri, and Roniko, your baby brother loves you dearly and thank you for being in my life.

7. To my father, Derry Haywood II, thank you for such a cool name and for being an example of going after what you want. I inherited that acute business acumen from you.

8. To my mother, Sara Haywood…thank you for being an amazing example of strength, faith, prayer, holiness, relentless warfare, and the unconditional love of Jesus Christ. You are living in the days where your children are rising up and calling you "Blessed!" You have prayed me through over the years and countless others. I am the product of your covenant with the father. Love you dearly…and always.

9. Saving the best for last, to my beautiful bride, best friend, partner, and co-captain in life Marquita. I love you so much and thank God every single day that he counted me worthy of the gift in you. We have known each other for over 30 years and each year I marvel how the father manages to knit us even tighter as the days go by. I couldn't imagine taking this journey without you and I stand in awe of who you have become in the Kingdom. You bear many titles as well however, to me you will always be "Mrs Wonderful. I love you with all my heart!

Introduction

This book is Volume One in a writing that is designed to put language to the realm of the apostolic movement. Not in denomination but in biblical function and design. There are many who are called to this work but are not sure how to identify the sign of this "kingdom insignia." When we arrive on earth we arrive with all that we need to accomplish the God given mandate and task upon all of our lives. Look at the etymology of a seed: it is composed of three parts: the embryo, endosperm and seed coat. The embryo is what will mature into a fully grown plant if placed in the right conditions, while the endosperm is a food supply for the developing plant. The seed coating protects the seed from pathogens and insects. The fully grown plant is already in the seed when it hits the ground. Who we are destined to be was already in us from the time we arrived into this world. (Romans 8: 28-30) *28 And we know that all things work together for good to them that love God, to them who are the called according to his purpose. 29 For whom he did foreknow, he also did **predestinate** to be conformed to the image of his Son, that he might be the firstborn among many brethren. 30 Moreover whom he did predestinate, them he also called: and whom he called, them he also justified: and whom he justified, them he also glorified.*

We have been predestined for a work and a call that is far beyond the identity we place upon ourselves. In Identity Discovery we hone in on the Identity God has placed within us to carry out HIs purpose. This is a reach that God does from within and the results are sure. When we

1

completely rely on God to complete the work he has begun we will see the full scope of our calls be made manifest openly. It cannot be denied, the authority, the passion, the forward throttle of the call will propel us into such a kingdom awareness. It is when yes is declared from our lips and our actions echo the same. Word and deed marry and God gives us the revelation of building his Kingdom by this apostolic oil and function.

Section 1

The Apostolic

Times have changed, culture has changed, the world is very fluid and unpredictable. As a matter of fact there is a term derived from the military that best identifies the terrain we are called to exist and win souls for Christ. That term is "VUCA." VUCA is an acronym that stands for Volatility, Uncertainty, Complexity, and Ambiguity. These are the conditions in which we now live which means this is the terrain we are called to build and plant in. How is this task possible? What tools must we use? What knowledge must we pull from to deliver the gospel in such a dynamic environment? It is going to take Apostolic mantles fully engaged to produce results in this type of climate. The next few sections outline the technology of this mantle and how it impacts the Kingdom of God and the origin of its intent in the earth.

Before we begin with the apostle we first have to visit the term "architect." Architect by definition is identified as *a person who is qualified to design buildings and to plan and supervise their construction.*

Looking at its very definition the first thing that stands out is **"a person qualified to design."** This identifies that walking in the apostolic requires certain qualifications, exposures and tenure in your craft or focus. There must be proven results.

They also are equipped with with several skills:

1. The "apostolic" is many things to many people however in researching this topic I was able to see the necessity for clarity to occur. Let's look at the definition and what the bible says about the Apostolic to get a further understanding of this calling.

apos· tle | \ ə-ˈpä-səl \

Definition of apostle

1: one sent on a mission: such as

> **a:** one of an authoritative New Testament group sent out to preach the gospel and made up especially of Christ's 12 original disciples and Paul
> **b:** the first prominent Christian missionary to a region or group St. Boniface, the Apostle of Germany

2: a person who initiates a great moral reform or who first advocates an important belief or system

> **a:** an ardent supporter: ADHERENT apostles of high technology

3: the highest ecclesiastical official in some church organizations

4: one of a Mormon administrative council of 12 men

ap· os· tol· ic | \ ˌa-pə-ˈstä-lik \

Definition of apostolic

1: of or relating to an apostle

a: of, relating to, or conforming to the teachings of the New Testament apostles

2: of or relating to a succession of spiritual authority from the apostles held (as by Roman Catholics, Anglicans, and Eastern Orthodox) to be perpetuated by successive ordinations of bishops and to be necessary for valid sacraments and orders

In looking at the definitions of both "Apostle and Apostolic we see some similarities in both implication and words. They are:

1. God's Authority
2. Sent Ones
3. Gospel Preaching and Teaching (Apologist)
4. Heavy Administrators
5. Initiators and Reformers
6. Mentors and Implementers of Succession

What is an Apostle?

The word "apostle" is recorded 19 times in 19 KJV verses, with its plural appearing an additional 60 times in 59 verses. It is derived from the Greek apostolos (Strong's Concordance #G652) which means someone who is a delegate or messenger, *one who is sent forth, or someone who is an ambassador of the Gospel.* The only place it is used twice in scripture is in 2 Corinthians where Paul gives a stern warning regarding those seeking to lead Christians astray.

The Bible does not limit the designation of "Apostle," a person specially sent to preach the gospel, only to the twelve men called and chosen by Jesus that we see in (Matthew 10:1-4, Mark 3:13-18). Paul's warning in 2 Corinthians 11:13 reveals others were given this holy calling and that they were **mimicked** by those seeking to take advantage of Christians. The original 12 disciples were, of course, unique as they were eyewitnesses to Jesus' earthly ministry (John 15:26-27). They heard his preaching to the people, saw his miracles, and so on. Although this naturally meant they had a certain authority in the teaching, they shared in the same responsibilities and spiritual gifts given to others with the same calling (i.e.Paul).

A man named Matthias was chosen by the eleven remaining disciples to take the place of Judas after his suicide (Acts 1:26). Paul and Barnabas are named apostles in the Bible in (Acts 14:14), as they were specially selected and sent by God to evangelize (Acts 13:1-3). Paul, in fact, had to vigorously defend his right to be considered an apostle based on his calling and the fruits it produced (1 Corinthians 9, Galatians 2).

This is an indicator that all will not acknowledge give credence to the call, however one must be able to **articulate and define their apostolic mandate.**

Biblical evidence additionally suggests Apollos (1Corinthian 4:6, 9), Silvanus and Timothy (1 Thessalonians 1:1, 2:6), as well as Andronicus (a possible distant relative of Paul's) and a person named Junia were also apostles (Romans 16:7). Paul referred to James, the Lord's physical half-brother, as also possessing this calling (Galatians 1:19).

"Apostolos" is translated "he that is sent" in John 13:16 where Jesus stated, ". . . neither he that is sent greater than he that sent him" (KJV). This is an indirect reference to himself as an Apostle, meaning someone sent by God the Father, which is confirmed in Hebrews 3:1. **Jesus Christ, was the first and is the Chief Apostle.**

The Apostolic Continued...

Paul the Apostle:

Since Paul had not accompanied Jesus during his earthly ministry, he did not meet the apostolic criteria of (Acts 1:21-22). It is clear, however, that he considered himself to be an apostle. Even though the only place in the Book of Acts where Paul is called an apostle is in reference to the apostles of the church in Antioch (Acts 14:4, 14), Luke's portrayal of

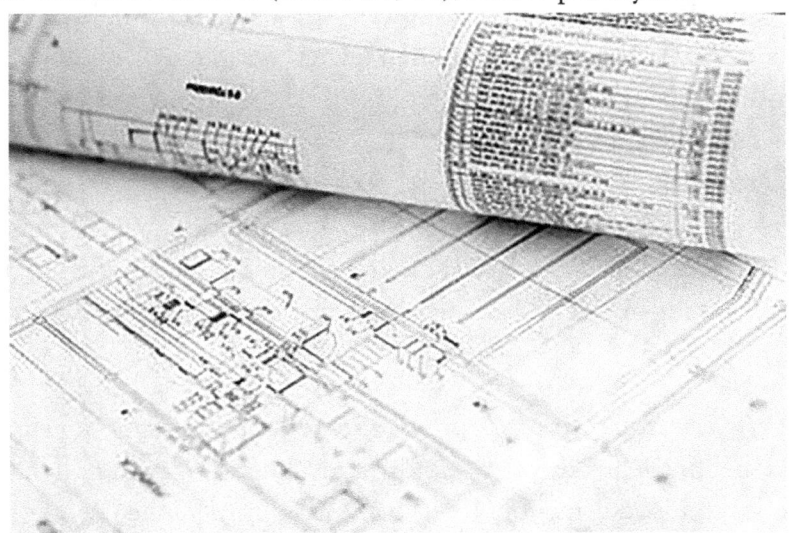

Paul's ministry as paradigmatic for the church gives implicit support to his apostolic claims. Not only does Acts depict Paul as manifesting the signs of an apostle, but in its three accounts of the Damascus Road encounter, his apostolic task is presented as the direct action of the risen Christ (9:3-5; 22:6-8; 26:12-18; cf. 2co 4:6; Gal 1:16).

Paul's own claim to apostleship is likewise based on the divine call of Christ (Rom 1:1; Col 1:1; Galatians 1:1 Galatians 1:15; cf. 2 Col 1:1; Eph 1:1; Col 1:1; 1 Tim 1:1; Tim 1:1; Titus 1:1). He is an apostle, "not from men nor by man, but *by Jesus Christ* and God the Father, who raised him from the dead" (Gal 1:1). His encounter with the resurrected Jesus served as the basis for his unique claim to be an "apostle to the Gentiles" (Rom 11:13). Paul bases his apostleship on the grace of God, not on ecstatic gifts or the signs of an apostle (2 Cor. 12). His apostolic commission is to serve God primarily through preaching the gospel (Rom 1:9; 15:19; 1 Col 1:17).

Paul uses the word "apostle" in more than one sense. At times he employs the term in the broader sense of messenger or agent (2 Col 8:23; Php 2:25). More often, however, Paul uses the term to refer to those who had been commissioned by the risen Lord to the apostolic task. Included in this category are the Twelve (although he never explicitly applies the title of apostle to them as a group), Peter (Gal 1:18), Paul himself (Rom 1:1; 1 Col 1:1; 9:1-2; 15:8-10; Gal 2:7-8), James the brother of Jesus (Gal 1:19; cf. Acts 15:13), Barnabas (1 Col 9:1-6; Gal 2:9; cf. Acts 14:4 Acts 14:14), and possibly others (Ro 16:7). In addition to understanding apostleship in terms of its basis in a divine call, Paul views the life of an apostle as being one of self-sacrificial service that entails suffering (1 Col 4:9-13; 15:30-32; 2 Col 4:7-12; 11:23-29).

The primary function of the apostles was to witness to Christ. The Twelve had intimate knowledge of his life, and a wider group had been witnesses to his resurrection. Their commissioning by the risen Lord to worldwide witness (Ac 1:8), however, was **incomplete without the anointing of the Spirit. Only after Pentecost were they empowered by the Spirit for their ministry of word and deed.** Their witness to Christ was not only empowered, but also guided and validated by the Spirit (John 14:26). **Thus, their full apostolic vocation was realized only in the Spirit** (John 14-17). Paul viewed apostleship as a gift of the Spirit (1 Co 12:28), which was often accompanied by miraculous signs and mighty works (2 Co 12:12). **Such signs and wonders, however, were clearly secondary to the apostolic functions of preaching and teaching.**

Apostolic Authority having direct knowledge of the incarnate Word, and being sent out as authorized agents of the gospel, the apostles provided the authentic interpretation of the life and teaching of Jesus.

Because their witness to Christ was guided by the Spirit (John 15:26-27) the apostles' teaching was considered normative for the church. They were regarded as the "pillars" (Gal 2:9) and "foundation" (Eph 2:20; cf. Rev 21:14) of the church, and their teaching became the norm for Christian faith and practice. **The deposit of revelation transmitted by the apostles and preserved in its** 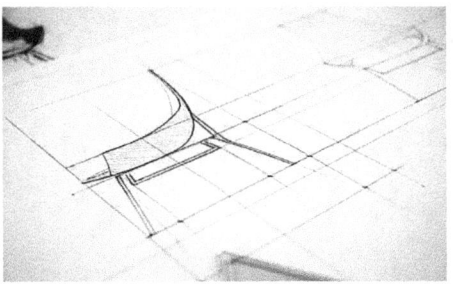 **written form in the New Testament thus forms the basis of postapostolic preaching and teaching in the church.**

It is evident that the apostles formed the nucleus of primitive Christianity. The New Testament highlights their function as apostles, without delineating in detail the authoritative nature of their office in relation to the church. What is emphasized is that their *apostolic commission authorized them to preach* (1 Co 1:17); t*o be ambassadors for Christ* (2 Col 5:20; Eph 6:20); *to be witnesses to all nations* (Luke 24:48); and t*o make disciples of all peoples* (Matt 28:19).

How do they function?

True Apostles are pioneers, gifted in innovation, structure, order, and government. They are trail blazers, pathfinders, architects, and they develop blueprints real-time to enhance the framework of the local church. They are disruptors, reformers and transformers who are gifted in systems and processes.

Section 2

They are apostolic in identity.

Untainted by the world. "And with many other words did he testify and exhort, saying, Save yourselves from this untoward generation." Acts 2:40 (KJV) "But ye are a chosen generation, a royal priesthood, an holy nation, a peculiar people; that ye should show forth the praises of him who hath called you out of darkness into his marvelous light;" 1 Peter 2:9 (KJV) Though they lived in the world, they identified not with it. They identified themselves with the culture of Christ, holy, set apart for His glory. Identity is the necessary component for any true apostolic leader in that it grounds the God given affirmation that produces a freedom to walk in and worthy of these callings to which we have been called. (Ephesians 4:1) Identity helps us not to just walk in it, but to walk **worthy** in it. We must gain an understanding in this discovery of identity that it is a privilege to serve in any capacity for Christ and that there is a worthiness that is associated with the call. Our walk must exemplify the excellency of the one who called us and therefore we must maintain carnal free living. We must fully embrace the call to fully receive the grace of the call. We see in the book of Jonah "Then the word of the Lord came to Jonah a second time, 'Go to the great city of Nineveh and proclaim to it the message I give you.'" This is an indicator that Jonah did not initially asap his call although he knew what was asked of him by God. Important point to grasp: True Apostolic callings don't just embrace the call, but they also **embrace the**

inconvenience of it. Our apostolic identity is one that will adjust regions but it must first adjust us.

Section 3

They are apostolic in commitment.

Everything belonged to the Lord. They went where the Lord told them to even when it meant facing their enemies and greatest persecutor. They gave sacrificially when they were instructed to. They used their talents for His glory. They lived in total abandonment to their Lord and Master. The Apostle must relinquish one's personal freedoms to be bound to Christ. Galatians 2:20 gives us the working blueprint for this task when it states, "I am crucified with Christ, nevertheless, I live." We must be dead men walking, deceased but living. Dead to our sin, dead to our opinions, dead to agendas, dead to rebellion and completely given over to Christ our example. It was Robin Mark who pinned the infamous, **"I Surrender All."** The lyrics embody the truth behind true apostolic commitment in the opening stanzas which state: *"All to Jesus I surrender, All to Thee I freely give. I will ever love and trust You, in Your presence daily live.* Jesus Christ, the Chief Apostle, must have not a fraction of us, but all of us. Pseudo commitment creates barriers and blockage in our ability to flow in our assignments. We must always be mindful of our commitment to God and thus display it! Yes is not just spoken, but it must be demonstrated in our daily lives.

Section 4

They are apostolic in devotion.

Act 2:42 gives us the insight for this apostolic value, its states; "And they continued steadfastly in the apostles' **doctrine** and **fellowship**, and in **breaking of bread**, and **in prayers.**" Despite persecution, **they neglected not their meeting together. Their worship was extravagant and with utter obedience.** The word was their foundation and the final authority. All things were wrought by prayer and conquered with the power of the word and spirit. This devotion spreads to the areas of **doctrine, fellowship, breaking of bread**, and in **prayer**. First we see **doctrine** mentioned. In its Greek origin it is cited as didaché - which means

teaching, a summarized body of respected teaching in the formal sense. The Apostles doctrine is concise teaching yet it must be respected teaching. It cannot be of-self or self-initiated, or self-promoting. It is the ancient writings given to us through the gospels and must be sustained throughout time by those who profess this doctrine, we the Apostolic. Now let's add clarity to this verbiage, this is not to be confused with denominational doctrine, this is bigger than a religious entity or organizational standard of belief. This is a **kingdom pathway**. This is the road that must be taken that highlights the message of the cross, its cost to redemption for us all, and the "finished work of Christ. Secondly **"fellowship"** is called out in this passage. In the Greek "koinōnia" is translated **communion, association, partnership**, from koinos common. Being apostolic in devotion means to provide opportunity for connection and fellowship. Authentic connection is a foundational core value of the kingdom of God, it stems from covenant. Jehovah is a God of covenant. A covenant is an agreement or a promise made between two partners who are striving together toward a common goal.

In the bible, God makes covenants with Noah, Abraham, and the people of Israel. In the New Testament, God makes a covenant with those who put their trust in Jesus to forgive their sins, ratifying the agreement with Christ's blood. God made a promise to Noah to maintain his relationship with creation, by not destroying the earth with a flood again. God's unconditional promise was accompanied by the sign of the rainbow. "I establish my covenant with you, that never again shall all flesh be cut off by the waters of the flood, and never again shall there be a flood to destroy the earth" (Genesis 9:11).

God made a promise to Abraham to make him the father of a great nation. He was faithful to that covenant, even when Abraham and Sarah were old and barren having no children. "I will make of you a great nation, and I will bless you and make your name great, so that you will be a blessing. I will bless those who bless you, and him who dishonors you I will curse, and in you all the families of the earth shall be blessed" (Genesis 12:2-3).

God's covenant with Israel was to be their God and for them to be his people. He was faithful to that covenant, even when they were unfaithful to him. "Now therefore, if you will indeed obey my voice and keep my covenant, you shall be my treasured possession among all peoples, for all the earth is mine; and you shall be to me a kingdom of priests and a holy nation" (Exodus 19:5-6).

The New Covenant is an agreement between God and those who put their trust in Jesus. It is ratified with Christ's blood. "In the same way he took the cup, after supper, saying, 'This cup is the new covenant in my blood. Do this, as often as you drink it, in remembrance of me'" (1 Corinthians 11:25).

This covenant promises us forgiveness, eternal life, and the indwelling of the Holy Spirit. The covenants teach us that God is faithful. He keeps his promises, even when we are unfaithful to him. We can count on God to uphold his promises because he is a convent keeping God!!!

Section 5

They are apostolic in their mission.

Their mission was the world. They were not satisfied with their home, town or city. They burned with a vision and desire to see the whole world evangelized.

They were apostolic in reaching the lost. Every day, they sought out the hungry and the thirsty. The Lord working with them, they expounded the word to some and to others, prayed and ministered to their needs. Everybody was a minister. There were not an **elite** few. The responsibility of reaching the lost belonged to every believer. The mission is apostolic in nature because it requires the "sending" of one for it to be executed. The "mission" is submerged in the Great "Com**mission.**" (Matthew 28:18-20) *Then Jesus came to them and said, "All authority in heaven and on earth has been given to Me.* Therefore go and make disciples of all nations, baptizing them in the name of the Father, and of the Son, and of the HolySpirit, and teaching them to obey all that I have commanded you. *And surely I am with you always, even to the end of the age." Commission by its very origin is derived from the word "commit or entrust." WE must commit ourselves to the Mission!*

Let's look at it like this:

1. **Commission** - an instruction, command, or duty given to a person or group of people.

2. **Mission** - an important assignment carried out for political, religious, or commercial purposes, typically involving travel.
3. **Omission** - a person or thing that has been left out or excluded.

All three words are present within the one. So here is the synopsis... within the Great **Commission** is a **Mission** that must be done without any **Omission** of anyone! When we add the prefix **"Co"** we gain a greater understanding that it must be done **"together."**

Section 6

They are apostolic in demonstrating the power and the love of God.

Signs, miracles and wonders confirmed the word. **They preached with authority and demonstration of the spirit.** Their life was lived with a passionate love for God and people. They allowed the Holy Ghost to live through them, exhibiting fruit for the world to see and taste the goodness of God.

The believers in the 1st Century were united and in harmonious fellowship with each other provided that their doctrine was consistent and pure. As a church, they had a structure that empowered every believer to offer their God-given gifts and talents in service to His body. In small gatherings, they were cared for by fellow believers who were governed by the five-fold ministry led by Jesus Christ. **Through the five-fold ministry, saints were equipped to do the work of the ministry. The church consisted of people belonging to different races and backgrounds brought together by one quest – to seek His kingdom and be a holy nation!** Despite difficult circumstances, they knew they were not alone. They had the backing of Almighty God and that was all that mattered. Their attitude? If God is for us, who can be against us? Heaven is their home and earth their passing through.

The mission and the purpose of the church has not changed. God is looking for earth partners. Until His coming and till we all come in the unity of the faith, and of the knowledge of the Son of God, unto a perfect man, unto the measure of the stature of the fulness of Christ, we continue the Acts of the Apostles with passion, purity and fervency. Apostles operate in power! One of my favorite scriptures in the whole bible is found in (Luke 10:19) it states, *Behold, I give unto you power to tread on serpents and scorpions, and over all the power of the enemy: and nothing shall by any means hurt you.* We must be apostolic in demonstrating power. What sets us apart from the rest is the fact that we bare the signs that accompany the Great Commission. (Mark 16:17-18) *And these signs shall follow them that believe; In my name shall they cast out devils; they shall speak with new tongues; They shall take up serpents; and if they drink any deadly thing, it shall not hurt them; they shall lay hands on the sick, and they shall recover.* When we are apostolic in demonstration of power, then we see freedom delivered to those who are bound under demonic oppression. An apostolic anointing breaks the power of the yoke, produces miracles in the presence of opposition and always gives the glory to God.

My Personal Experience:

In studying the "apostolic mantle" and the apostles it gave me the precursor I needed to look into my own life and trace the origins of this gift that up until now lay dormant. Looking into retrospect, I realized that my first act was founding Freedom Church United, Inc. Planting a church from ground zero is not for the faint of heart. I moved from my familiar place into a city where I knew no one, and no one knew me. I would often ask God why not just stay where I know people, and have a family present. In my mind that would have made sense and would have been so much easier. However that was not the intent of the Father. So I went to a foreign city and began to dig a new work and lay a new foundation for liberation and freedom to be housed within Richmond VA, (RVA), Freedom Church United, which Bishop SY Younger affectionately calls (Freedom Church International)...loI

I had no blueprint, no rubric, because I was the first to plant in my area of influence. My covering at the time never planted anything; they only enhanced what previously existed. I can remember writing out systems and programs that would exist 15 years ago that we are now just beginning to implement. Seeing beyond the scope of now and gazing into what would be, that's a part of being apostolic. I noticed the signs of regional authority first in the spirit. I would travel to cities and regions and pick up the "strongmen" or governing authority of the area. I would go to people's houses (churches) and feel what things would "squat" there in the spirit. My perspective on the word shifted. I now see the word as a rubric as opposed to an instruction manual. It is a tool of "evaluation" as well as instruction. It measures the apostolic in you! Evaluation is the process initiated to critically examine a program. Apostolic mantles are sent not only to build however, but to **examine what is preexisting with the word of God as his rubric, adjusting the house as needed.** My sight became clearer and my discernment heightened as I could sense the shift of my dominate "Fivefold" gifting. I could see things in leadership (anywhere) but could say nothing about what I saw. Both the good and things that had an opportunity to improve. I would pray and ask God for direction and what to do with the information. He would grace me with the words to pray or even speak with that individual should opportunity be presented.

Section 7

My Mandate and Marketplace

In the marketplace, I was given the gift of leadership, I taught it, understood it and began to build leaders in the marketplace. I created systems and stood up operations centers, much like how Freedom House was stood up from ground zero. Endurance was now gifted because I knew that some results took time:

- I remained consistent and functioned in sticktoitiveness
- My words carry unusual weight and authority, and I noticed I could positively challenge policy and it would adjust and change to my consideration. God had given me "sway." Sway is a pillar of dominion which I highlight in my next release "Decree!"
- He began to give me audiences with men of power and affluence, I was no longer just in the room, but I had been given a voice in the room.

An "Executive Oil" had been released....we will revisit this concept in a few I was a dedicated security professional with 15 plus years of security experience and over 18 years in leadership development and training. I saw myself serve as a critical point of contact between Enterprise Security and organizational lines of business (LOB's), providing advice and solutions that mitigate operational, strategic, tactical and technical risk. I was known to have a reputation for being consistent and maintaining an optimistic viewpoint in varying environments while delivering impactful and valuable outcomes. I mastered Project Management, analyzing business-critical data to identify inefficiencies and trends in projects, which prevents issues from arising, enabling seamless project execution. I created and implemented contingency plans, defining roadmaps, and providing periodic recommendations.

Leading in the Market place continued...

I had a God given effectiveness in managing complex people, process and technical projects able to assess all situations and keen skills. I initiated theoretical, managerial, and technical skills to fulfill identified objectives and deliverables and created a solid project management strategy for task interdependence. Managing project risks, contingency and mitigation plans while maintaining high team performance, productivity & benchmarking.

Back to Executive Oil:

What is an Executive Oil?

For us to truly understand this concept lets define executive.

What is an executive ?

A business executive is a senior-level employee who manages an organization and makes decisions to help it grow. They are often the public face of the company. They make up the "C-suite. The C-suite is a term for the top executives in a company, and the most influential positions in an organization. The "C" stands for "chief", which is the first letter of many C-suite titles, such as CEO and CFO. Some of the responsibilities are:

Responsibilities

- **Create plans**: Develop strategies to help the company grow

- **Make decisions**: Oversee budgets, negotiate contracts, and analyze sales reports
- **Manage people**: Recruit, hire, train, and promote staff
- **Build relationships**: Work with employees, customers, and other stakeholders
- **Represent the company**: Serve as the company's public face
- **Embrace change**: Encourage innovation and new ideas

Now, let's take a look at the C-Suite of the Bible, these are some of the executives of the kingdom who moved in seats of power and senior leadership grace.

1. **Paul** – Paul met with governmental officials, challenged systems, and evangelized to seats of power, He carried an executive oil As an apostle and missionary, Paul executed the Great Commission with zeal, spreading the gospel throughout the Roman Empire, empowering the early church (Acts 13:2-3). He also wrote many epistles, guiding believers with profound leadership and doctrine (2 Timothy 4:2).
2. **Moses** – Moses was appointed by God to lead the Israelites out of Egypt, displaying executive leadership in delivering the law and establishing the covenant with God, as outlined in Exodus 3:10-12 and Deuteronomy 34:10-12.
3. **Joseph** – Joseph's executive role as second-in-command in Egypt, managing resources during famine, exemplified wisdom and foresight. His leadership was rooted in faithfulness, as seen in Genesis 41:46 and 50:20.
4. **Barnabas** – Barnabas, a key leader in the early church, displayed leadership through encouragement, mentorship, and support for Paul (Acts 9:27, Acts 11:25-26), executing God's will by strengthening believers and expanding the kingdom.
5. **Joshua** – Joshua was in the presence of God. A theophany had taken place in Joshua 5:15: "The commander of the Lord's army said to

Joshua, "Remove the sandals from your feet, for the place where you are standing is holy." And Joshua did so." Due his special blessing, he was appointed as one with judicial powers and responsibilities in Joshua 14:6-15. As Moses' successor, Joshua led the Israelites into the Promised Land, executing God's plans with courage and obedience (Joshua 1:6-9). His leadership marked a pivotal shift in the conquest of Canaan.

6. **Ruth** – Ruth, though not in a traditional executive role, demonstrated powerful leadership through her loyalty and faith, leading to her marriage to Boaz and becoming part of the lineage of King David, as seen in Ruth 1:16-17 and Ruth 4:13-17.

7. **Nehemiah** – Nehemiah exhibited excellent executive leadership in rebuilding Jerusalem's walls, inspiring the people to action despite opposition, as recorded in Nehemiah 2:17-18 and 4:6.

8. **Peter** – As the leader of the early church, Peter was entrusted with the role of guiding the apostles, preaching boldly, and making pivotal decisions, particularly at the Jerusalem Council (Matthew 16:18-19, Acts 15:7-11).

9. **Noah** – Noah executed God's command by building the ark, saving his family and the animals from the flood, serving as a faithful servant in a corrupt world, as seen in Genesis 6:14-22 and Genesis 9:1-17.

10. **Deborah** – As a prophetess and judge, Deborah executed leadership in Israel by guiding the people spiritually and militarily, leading them to victory over their enemies (Judges 4:4-9, Judges 5:7). Her wisdom and courage were key to Israel's deliverance.

Why did I take the time to run through this seemingly resume at this point in the chapter is because these operational, managerial, and leadership tasks are all possible because of my apostolic mantle and mandate. It was the apostolic grit that pushed me to build systems in the marketplace. It enabled me to establish order and succession, legislating within my own metron and pulling the hidden potential out of those under my purview. My personal Apostloic Mandate can be broken down into 3 major themes. I have been called to expand the kingdom and the winning of souls utilizing all of the gifts afforded me however they are concentrated within these 3 pillars.

1. Disruption:
2. Innovation:
3. Kingdom:

Disruption (of a company or form of technology) means to cause radical change in (an industry or market) by means of innovation. So then what is innovation? Innovation is making changes in something established, especially by introducing new methods, ideas, or products. Let's look at bible, (Exodus 35:30-35)

31 And Moses said unto the children of Israel, See, the Lord hath called by name Bezaleel the son of Uri, the son of Hur, of the tribe of Judah;

*32 And **he hath filled him with the spirit of God**, in wisdom, in understanding, and in knowledge, and in all manner of workmanship;*

*33 And **to devise curious works**, to work in gold, and in silver, and in brass, 33 And in the cutting of stones, to set them, and in carving of wood, to make any manner of cunning work.*

34 And he hath put in his heart that he may teach, both he, and Aholiab, the son of Ahisamach, of the tribe of Dan.

35 Them hath he filled with wisdom of heart, to work all manner of work, of the engraver, and of the cunning workman, and of the embroiderer, in blue, and in purple, in scarlet, and in fine linen, and of the weaver, even of them that do any work, and of those that devise cunning work.

This text provides direct credence to the anointing of innovation that's necessary to build for God versus ourselves. The "Message" translation unlocks it further: (Exodus 35:30-35) *30-35 Moses told the Israelites, "See, God has selected Bezalel son of Uri, son of Hur, of the tribe of Judah. **He's filled him with the Spirit of God, with skill, ability, and know-how for making all sorts of things, to design and work in gold, silver, and bronze; to carve stones and set them; to carve wood, working in every kind of skilled craft.** And he's also made him a teacher, he and Oholiab son of Ahisamach, of the tribe of Dan. He's gifted them with the know-how needed for carving, designing, weaving, and embroidering in blue, purple, and scarlet fabrics, and in fine linen. They can make anything and design anything."*

It is God who equips with the calling of Innovation and every crafty skill to build for His Kingdom. I have begun to embrace this calling to further enhance what God has called me to do, and partner with those who are a part of the same tribe of Disruptors and Innovators. **The artisans and divine designers of this current time.** I use to run from this call for many seasons not knowing how to properly articulate what it is or what it means.

In this season, I understand it, can articulate it, and have already begun operating in it. This is only the beginning, more lies ahead and God is the chief innovator. He is always adjusting the scope while maintaining the overall mission…Seek and Save the Lost!!! The Lord will download heaven's intelligence to his leaders to work new technologies and extend greater resources to cause ministry work load to become lighter. It becomes embedded within the individual's DNA. The apostle's DNA is signature in its own right; it looks like nothing else within the 5 fold. The genetic code stems directly from heaven authentication. This is why the apostles are affirmed! This affirmation does not make them an apostle as much as it identifies and calls out what has been already deposited by God. It is not an **office** such as a bishop which is initiated through the liturgy of consecration however, it is a heavenly function with a completing priority to the bishopric not a competing priority. I will outline this more in volume 2, "Identity Discovery, the DNA of the Apostle."

Section 8

The Apostolic Mandate and Matrix

The Mandate

Apostles function in Executive Capacity!" They move with an executive presence, which essentially means they have the innate ability to inspire confidence! They carry both the **mandate of leadership** and the **matrix of leadership.** When we look at Paul in scripture, although he never sat in the seat of "Lead Pastor," he was a carrier of both the mandate of leadership and the matrix of leadership. Let's take a look at the mandate. (Romans 1:1-4) KJV states: *1 Paul, a servant of Jesus Christ, called to be an apostle, separated unto the gospel of God, 2 (Which he had promised afore by his prophets in the holy scriptures,) 3 Concerning his Son Jesus Christ our Lord, which was made of the seed of David according to the flesh; 4 And declared to be the Son of God with power, according to the spirit of holiness, by the resurrection from the dead:*

(1 Corinthians 1:1-4) KJV states: *1 Paul called to be an apostle of Jesus Christ through the will of God, and Sosthenes our brother, 2 Unto the church of God which is at Corinth, to them that are sanctified in Christ Jesus, called to be saints, with all that in every place call upon the name of Jesus Christ our Lord, both theirs and our's: 3 Grace be unto you, and peace, from God our Father, and from the Lord Jesus Christ. 4 I thank my God always on*

your behalf, for the grace of God which is given you by Jesus Christ; Within these 2 passages of scripture we see a common theme to this salutation from Paul. It lies within the statement bolded in both passages that states: "Called to be an Apostle!" Herein lies the root mandate! A mandate is an official order or commission to carry out a specific task. Paul is clear of his God given mandate and identity thus informing the churches that he is called a guardian not just of the local churches, but of the Gospel itself. He's called to calibrate the church and how she (the bride) responds to the gospel they must so graciously carry, preach, and live by. Paul here moves as a kingdom executive, or a person with senior managerial responsibility in an organization. An executive connotes having the power to put plans, actions, or laws into effect. He announces his authority and therefore proceeds forward in correction, reproof, rebuke, exaltation, and training in righteousness.

Understanding the Apostolic: The Apostolic is Broad

Understanding what it is…

- **Apostolic Graces:**
    - Building, Apologist in Gospel Preaching, Order Setters, Innovation Agents, Masters of Controlled Disruption,
- **Apostolic Agilities:**
    - **Leadership Agilities:** Simply put, leadership agility is the ability to effectively lead organizational change, build teams, and navigate challenging business conversations.
    - **Apostolic Agilities:** Lead Change, Build Teams, and Navigate Confronting Apologetic Conversations, Regional Response, Executive presence, Jurisdiction and magistrate authority
- **Apostolic Technologies:**
    - Deeper realms of prayer, the prophetic, Kingdom blueprints, the artisan anointing, ancient oil,

- ▶ What is technology in your own definition?
  - – Technology is the use of scientific knowledge for practical purposes or applications, whether in industry or in our everyday lives.
- **Apostolic Intelligence:**
  - ■ Intel is a security term which means this information is for the believer who is ready to take action: You do not need Intel to do nothing…

Intelligence is not knowing something, it's finding something. This is office and predictive and actionable. You have to know how to navigate in the prophetic and search the word for solutions.

What is the Matrix?

- Matrices are used whenever one needs to represent in a short form an infinite or finite collection of some entities arranged in rows and columns.
- The Matrix of the apostolic deals with his or her ability to foster and awaken the gifts within the body of Christ. It requires the release of a divine endowment

The Matrix

In the etymology of the word Matrix we see that it is related to the Latin word for "mother," originally meant "pregnant animal" or "breeding female" and **was later generalized to mean "womb."** Today, matrix includes any nurturing or supportive setting or substance usually within the fields of math and the sciences

The Matrix of the apostolic deals with his or her ability to foster and awaken the gifts within the body of Christ. It requires the release of a divine endowment, that is to be awakened from incubation and then brought forth by a "sent one." Only apostolic mantles can activate and awaken from incubation. *(2 Timothy 1:6) Paul reminds Timothy to "fan the flame" or to stir him through the laying on of hands, urging him to actively use and grow his spiritual gifts. Paul was pulling out of Timothy what was in incubation. The Apostolic Matrix of the Kingdom enables us to house infinite possibilities and giftings. It is a gaze into capacity consciousness, it is a short representation representing and infinite amount of possibilities.*

It is my prayer that this series forward thrust us into a greater dimension of who we have been called to be as apostolic leaders. Building but first tearing down when necessary, uplifting but razing simultaneously, planting yet uprooting. It's the culture of the call and we must be ambidextrous in our ability to build in these various types of terrain. We must tumultuously plow with the grace of God and a relentless sticktoitiveness so that we will reap the harvest entrusted to those skilled in building the kingdom of God. Jesus is coming and we must be ready for the Chief Apostle's return. **Now...Let's Build!!!**

Section 9

My I.D

Understanding your ID is vital because much like in the natural ID is necessary for day to day living and access. In general, "ID" or an identification document is used to prove your identity or age, and can be required for various purposes like accessing secure facilities, boarding flights, and interacting with government agencies.

Here's a more detailed breakdown:

Common Uses of Identification Documents (IDs):

Proving Identity and Age:
IDs like driver's licenses, state-issued IDs, and passports are used to verify who you are and your age.

Accessing Secure Facilities:
IDs are often required to enter secure areas like government buildings, military bases, and airports.

Boarding Flights:
You will need a REAL ID-compliant driver's license or another accepted form of ID to board domestic flights.

Interacting with Government Agencies:
IDs are necessary for various government transactions, including applying for benefits, registering to vote, and obtaining licenses.

Financial Transactions:
IDs are required for opening bank accounts, applying for credit, and other financial activities.

Purchasing Age-Restricted Items:
IDs are used to verify age when purchasing alcohol or tobacco.

Other Purposes:
IDs can be required for signing contracts, registering at schools or universities, and other situations where verification is needed.

Now in parallel to these requirements our ID in the supernatural is just as key. Without knowing who were are we will never be able to have the proper access or walk in realms of power. Our ID in the spirit provides:

Proving Identity and Age:
The spirit realm requires identification of belonging and of tenure. Let's look at an example in Acts. The Bible, specifically in Acts 19:13-16, recounts an incident where seven sons of a Jewish high priest named Sceva attempted to exorcise a demon-possessed man by invoking the name of Jesus, but were instead overpowered and fled the house naked and wounded.

Here's a more detailed explanation:

The Incident:
Some Jewish exorcists, including the seven sons of Sceva, tried to cast out a demon using the name of Jesus, claiming to do so by the authority of Paul's teachings.

The Demon's Response:
The demon, however, recognized Jesus and Paul, but not the sons of Sceva, and violently attacked them, causing them to flee the house in a state of disarray.

The Outcome:
The incident became widely known in Ephesus, causing fear among both Jews and Greeks, and ultimately, the name of Jesus was magnified.

Here we can plainly see the significance of knowing who you are. When imposters try to operate within Kingdom jurisdiction it creates both an unfruitful and embarrassing situation. Don't be an imposter, know who you are and operate within that realm of authority that has been assigned to you!

Accessing Secure Facilities:
ID is necessary because certain access requires you to be ID'ed to make sure you are supposed to be where you are trying to access. Lets look at "access" more granularly.

ACCESS

ak'-ses (prosagoge, "a leading to or toward," "approach"):

Shown 3 times in the New Testament to indicate the acceptable way of approach to God and of admission to His favor. Jesus said, "I am the way" (**John 14:6**). His blood is the "new and living way" (**Hebrews 10:20**). Only through Him have we "access by faith into this grace wherein we stand" (**Romans 5:2**); "Through him we both have access by one Spirit unto the Father" (**Ephesians 2:18** the King James Version); "in whom we have .... access in confidence, through our faith in him" (**Ephesians 3:12**).

The goal of redemption is life in God, "unto the Father." The means of redemption is the cross of Christ, "in whom we have our redemption through his blood" (**Ephesians 1:7**). The agent in redemption is the Holy Spirit, "by one Spirit," "sealed with the Holy Spirit of promise" (**Ephesians 1:13**). The human instrumentality, faith. The whole process of approach to, and abiding fellowship with, God is summed up in this brief formula:

Access to the Father: through Christ, by the Spirit, by faith = Access!

Boarding Flights:
Boarding flights simply mean traveling in the realm of the spirit. Having your ID is crucial when we are navigating new spaces in the supernatural. We travel in the spirit through at least 3 major access points:

1. Dreams - in our subconscious state
   a. The Bible mentions dreams and visions as a means of divine communication, with passages like **Joel 2:28** stating that God will pour out his Spirit on all people, and that old men will dream dreams and young men will see visions. However, it's also cautioned to test the validity of such dreams and visions, ensuring they align with God's Word.
2. Visions - in our conscious state awake and aware
   a. **Revelation 1:9-10**
      9) I John, who also am your brother, and companion in tribulation, and in the kingdom and patience of Jesus Christ, was in the isle that is called Patmos, for the word of God, and for the testimony of Jesus Christ. 10) I was in the Spirit on the Lord's day, and heard behind me a great voice, as of a trumpet,
3. Prayer - through the lens of the Holy Spirit
   a. Prayer is one of the tools that enables you to access into the supernatural, when you pray you open a line of communication with God and connect directly with Him, prayer makes the

impossible possible, there are certain levels in the spiritual realm you'll never get to if you don't pray and develop consistent relational practices. **Daniel 10** highlights the fervent prayer of Daniel that accesses the "angelic commander" in the heavens who wrestled the Prince of Persia.

No matter the access point they all require proper identification for us to access. When we access these points without proper credentials we are illegal and must submit to God's vetting process. It is possible to tap into realms by a dark authority. Stay away from any power that does not require submission and consecration to Jesus Christ…this is a whole other teaching.

Interacting with Government Agencies:
Our identity gives us access to Government! When you know who you are you become aware of your jurisdiction. We spoke in a previous chapter about having "executive presence" and an oil for audiences with men of power. Paul embarked on four main missionary journeys, traveling about 9,150 miles in 14 years. His willingness to travel great distances to preach of Christ helped establish Christianity throughout the Mediterranean. Paul visited cities across the Roman Empire to bring the Savior's message not only to the Jews but also to the Gentiles: "I strived to preach the gospel, not where Christ was named" (Romans 15:20). His jurisdiction gave him access to governmental power and access to the "kings of men."

I think we get the picture at this point…When you discover your identity in Christ it is the breeding ground for all kinds of access to the supernatural and to places the kingdom needs to penetrate. This is why the enemy does not want you to know who you are. If you ever grabbed hold to you "ID" you would have proof and authority to move into realms of power that bring about manifestation in the earth.

Section 10

Steps to Discovery:

How do we practically discover what is within? Here are some practical steps that helped me and I pray they will help you as well.

Step 1: Seek God First Through Prayer and the Word

To understand your identity in God's kingdom, start by seeking God through prayer and reading His Word. The Bible is the primary source for knowing who you are in Christ and how God views you.

- **Scripture References:**
  - *Matthew 6:33* – "But seek first the kingdom of God and His righteousness, and all these things will be added to you."
  - *Jeremiah 29:13* – "You will seek me and find me when you seek me with all your heart."
  - *Psalm 119:105* – "Your word is a lamp to my feet and a light to my path."

Step 2: Understand Your Identity in Christ

Your true identity is found in Christ. When you accept Jesus as your Lord and Savior, you become a new creation, and your identity shifts from who you were to who you are in Him.

- **Scripture References:**
  - ► *2 Corinthians 5:17* – "Therefore, if anyone is in Christ, he is a new creation; the old has gone, the new has come."
  - ► *Ephesians 2:10* – "For we are God's workmanship, created in Christ Jesus to do good works, which God prepared in advance for us to do."
  - ► *Galatians 2:20* – "I have been crucified with Christ and I no longer live, but Christ lives in me. The life I now live in the body, I live by faith in the Son of God, who loved me and gave himself for me."

Step 3: Know Your Purpose Through God's Calling

Every believer has a unique purpose within God's kingdom. Understanding your purpose requires listening for God's call in your life, which will align with His will and glory. God has given each of us spiritual gifts and talents to serve others.

- **Scripture References:**
  - ► *Romans 8:28* – "And we know that in all things God works for the good of those who love him, who have been called according to his purpose."
  - ► *Ephesians 4:1* – "As a prisoner for the Lord, then, I urge you to live a life worthy of the calling you have received."
  - ► *1 Peter 4:10* – "Each of you should use whatever gift you have received to serve others, as faithful stewards of God's grace in its various forms."

Step 4: Recognize Your Authority and Inheritance in Christ

In Christ, you are not only a servant but also an heir of God's kingdom. Realizing your authority in Christ allows you to walk in confidence, overcoming obstacles and standing firm against spiritual attacks.

- **Scripture References:**
  - ▶ *Romans 8:17* – "Now if we are children, then we are heirs—heirs of God and co-heirs with Christ, if indeed we share in his sufferings in order that we may also share in his glory."
  - ▶ *Luke 10:19* – "I have given you authority to trample on snakes and scorpions and to overcome all the power of the enemy; nothing will harm you."
  - ▶ *John 1:12* – "Yet to all who did receive him, to those who believed in his name, he gave the right to become children of God."

Step 5: Walk in Faith and Obedience to God's Leading

As you grow in understanding of your identity, the next step is to walk in obedience to the Holy Spirit's leading. God will direct your steps and guide you toward fulfilling His destiny for you.

- **Scripture References:**
  - ▶ *Proverbs 3:5-6* – "Trust in the Lord with all your heart and lean not on your own understanding; in all your ways submit to him, and he will make your paths straight."
  - ▶ *Romans 12:2* – "Do not conform to the pattern of this world, but be transformed by the renewing of your mind. Then you will be able to test and approve what God's will is—his good, pleasing and perfect will."
  - ▶ *Galatians 5:16* – "So I say, walk by the Spirit, and you will not gratify the desires of the flesh."

Step 6: Embrace Your Kingdom Assignment

Each believer has a unique role in God's kingdom. As you step into your identity, embrace the assignment God has for you, whether in ministry, family, work, or other spheres of influence. Trust that God has positioned you to make an impact for His kingdom.

- **Scripture References:**
  - ▶ *Matthew 28:19-20* – "Therefore go and make disciples of all nations, baptizing them in the name of the Father and of the Son and of the Holy Spirit, and teaching them to obey everything I have commanded you. And surely I am with you always, to the very end of the age."
  - ▶ *2 Timothy 4:5* – "But you, keep your head in all situations, endure hardship, do the work of an evangelist, discharge all the duties of your ministry."
  - ▶ *Colossians 3:23* – "Whatever you do, work at it with all your heart, as working for the Lord, not for human masters."

Step 7: Live in Kingdom Authority, Power, and Love

Living out your identity and destiny requires recognizing that you are an ambassador of Christ, called to reflect His power, authority, and love in everything you do.

- **Scripture References:**
  - ▶ *Matthew 10:1* – "Jesus called his twelve disciples to him and gave them authority to drive out impure spirits and to heal every disease and sickness."
  - ▶ *Romans 15:13* – "May the God of hope fill you with all joy and peace as you trust in him, so that you may overflow with hope by the power of the Holy Spirit."
  - ▶ *1 John 4:16* – "So we have come to know and to believe the love that God has for us. God is love. Whoever abides in love abides in God, and God abides in them."

Step 8: Continually Grow and Mature in Your Relationship with God

Identity discovery is an ongoing process. As you walk with God, you will continue to learn more about who He is and who He has created you to be. Spiritual maturity allows you to walk confidently in your purpose and fulfill your kingdom calling.

- **Scripture References:**
  - ▸ *Ephesians 4:15* – "Instead, speaking the truth in love, we will grow to become in every respect the mature body of him who is the head, that is, Christ."
  - ▸ *2 Peter 3:18* – "But grow in the grace and knowledge of our Lord and Savior Jesus Christ. To him be glory both now and forever! Amen."
  - ▸ *Philippians 1:6* – "Being confident of this, that he who began a good work in you will carry it on to completion until the day of Christ Jesus."

This is not the absolute formula it is will definitely lead you to the path of your personal identity discovery. As I close this segment of the "Identity Series" I want to decree one word over your life that will unlock you to greater purpose and pathways to your ID. I decree over you "Discover!"

- Discover you define destiny in Jesus Christ
- Discover your place amongst the great men and women of the faith
- Discover your kingdom jurisdiction
- Discover your personal mandate
- Discover your inner you that is waiting to be unlocked
- Discover your opportunities to impact society
- Discover your abilities they have been untapped
- Discover your range of impact
- Discover you role within the body of Christ

And finally…Discover your Kingdom Identity and own what you find through the navigation of the Holy Spirit!

In Jesus Name!

Section 11
Ascension Prayer:

Father, I thank you for the joy of my salvation and the finished work of Jesus Christ. It is because you were sent as the first apostle that provided the template for the rest of us to adhere to. Prepare this vessel to walk at the next level of grace and continue to cultivate within me the genetic makeup of the Apostle. Wash me true and wash me whole that there remains none of the old man, old habits, or old mindsets from the previous season. I profess that all things have become new! Build me into the builder you have predestined for me to be. Grace me with the language of kingdom architecture, the call of the artisan, and the cry of the clarion to maintain and carry the weight of this great task. I will see to it that I continue to die daily and let the luminous light of Jesus Christ be seen through me. Regardless of the terrain, regardless of the encounter, regardless of the platform…the Glory will always remain with you. Grant me the support system of Nehemiah that I may stay on the wall, and grant me the resources of Persia that all I put my hands to do will be accomplished fiscally. Build within me the government of God, and sharpen my insight and discernment to see beyond what is said. This is only the beginning and I trust you to lead and guide for the entirety of the journey. You are my God, you are my King, and you are my Lord. I seal this prayer of ascension in the irreversible blood of Jesus, for its work cannot be undone…Amen